A STEP-BY-STEP BOOK ABOUT
GOLDFISH

JACK C. HARRIS

Photography:
Dr. Herbert R. Axelrod; Tom Caravaglia; D. Dady and E. Krygowski; Stanislav Frank; Michael Gilroy; courtesy of Midori Shobo, *Fish Magazine*, Japan; Klaus Paysan; Fred Rosenzweig; Andre Roth.

Humorous drawings by Andrew Prendimano.

Distributed in the UNITED STATES by T.F.H. Publications, Inc., 211 West Sylvania Avenue, Neptune City, NJ 07753; in CANADA to the Pet Trade by H & L Pet Supplies Inc., 27 Kingston Crescent, Kitchener, Ontario N2B 2T6; Rolf C. Hagen Ltd., 3225 Sartelon Street, Montreal 382 Quebec; in CANADA to the Book Trade by Macmillan of Canada (A Division of Canada Publishing Corporation), 164 Commander Boulevard, Agincourt, Ontario M1S 3C7; in ENGLAND by T.F.H. Publications Limited, 4 Kier Park, Ascot, Berkshire SL5 7DS; in AUSTRALIA AND THE SOUTH PACIFIC by T.F.H. (Australia) Pty. Ltd., Box 149, Brookvale 2100 N.S.W., Australia; in NEW ZEALAND by Ross Haines & Son, Ltd., 18 Monmouth Street, Grey Lynn, Auckland 2, New Zealand; in SINGAPORE AND MALAYSIA by MPH Distributors (S) Pte., Ltd., 601 Sims Drive, #03/07/21, Singapore 1438; in the PHILIPPINES by Bio-Research, 5 Lippay Street, San Lorenzo Village, Makati Rizal; in SOUTH AFRICA by Multipet Pty. Ltd., 30 Turners Avenue, Durban 4001. Published by T.F.H. Publications, Inc. Manufactured in the United States of America by T.F.H. Publications, Inc.

CONTENTS:

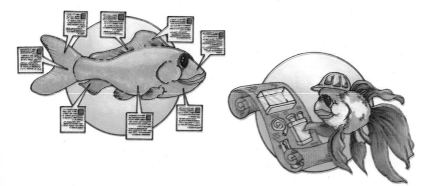

INTRODUCTION

Almost every household at one time or another enjoyed the company of one or more goldfish. Keeping goldfish is one of the most widespread and popular national hobbies. However, because they are so readily available and inexpensive, goldfish have become, unfortunately, an example of a "throwaway pet," since many owners, young and old, believe them to be short-lived. Their fascinating movements and aquatic beauty make them attractive to many pet buyers despite this reputation. Dispelling their negative notoriety is only one of the reasons this book is being written. Our other goals are to help new goldfish owners become familiar with the basic history, care, and feeding of their pets and to help undecided potential pet owners make a final and educated selection. In these pages you'll find that goldfish are actually hardy animals which, if properly cared for, enjoy long and contented lives displaying their beauty in aquariums or ponds.

As an introduction and overview, this book will bring together a wealth of information researched and gathered by fish scholars, breeders, and keepers from around the world. It will be a readily available guidebook and reference on goldfish. It is *not* intended to be a scientific work, but it will supply the answers to the majority of questions that new and potential goldfish owners need to have to enjoy the maximum pleasure from their pets. If pet owners do not find the answers to specific questions in this volume, we strongly recommend seeking the advice of your local pet shop owner. These people are the experts and will always be more than happy to help you with any particular problem you may experience when raising your pet goldfish.

FACING PAGE:
This Tigerhead Oranda is currently one of the most popular goldfish strains in the world.

Most of the animals that walk the earth and the fish that swim the sea have origins dating back to prehistoric times. Their development is traced through natural evidence such as fossils, using methods which are often challenged and constantly being revised. Although its true beginnings are cloaked in legend and mythology, the tiny goldfish enjoys a much shorter and more traceable origin. The goldfish, also known in some areas of the world as the Golden Carp, are a soft-finned species of fresh water fish. While it was in 1758, in von Linne's *Systema Naturae*, that the goldfish gained its scientific name, *Carassius auratus*, their centuries-long development has been better documented than that of most other animals. They belong to the family Cyprinidae and are relatively small, generally measuring about five to six inches long, although they often grow larger in captivity. As is the case with most other members of the Cyprinidae family, goldfish enjoy long lives, some re-

Chinese Lionheads have a shallower back profile than the Japanese *Ranchu*. This specimen has an attractive black edging to the caudal fins.

Introduction

This Redcap Oranda is a striking addition to any aquarium.

portedly living as long as 70 years.

Goldfish are originally native to eastern Asia, but they have been successfully bred throughout the world. The familiar fish we all know today are the product of inbreeding among different species with a good deal of aid from man. For centuries, goldfish have been bred by the Chinese, who taught their breeding techniques to the Japanese. These Chinese worked with mutations, exaggerating the more unusually attractive characteristics through many, many generations of fish over a span of many hundreds of years.

Chinese goldfish history consists of many different legendary origins, including a mystical beginning in a lake near the Chien-Ching Mountain in the ancient Province of Chekiang. Another popular myth speaks about the emergence of a goldfish from a magic well, marking the end of a devastating drought during the Chou Dynasty 750 years before the birth of Christ. This, many scholars believe, is merely a mention of the fish in mythology and not a supposed origin. Historic reference to goldfish breeders dates back to the Sung Dynasty from the 10th to the 13th century. There are some obscure and uncertain earlier references, but various Chinese writers of that time mention the *Chin Chi-yu* (goldfish).

Since the laws of genetics were not known until the Austrian monk and botanist Gregor Johann Mendel formulated them in 1865, it must be assumed that the Chinese worked, at first, with natural mutations of the Crucian Carp, selecting the more beautiful ones and breeding them together. The offspring produced by these breedings were again separated from the ordinary carp until, only a few generations later, large numbers of goldfish appeared among the offspring.

The wealthy Japanese were reported as having kept pet goldfish at the beginning of the 16th century until the breeders in Japan began meeting with success to such a degree as to make them available to the general populace. There were, and still are, many goldfish competitions and fairs held in Japan.

Really show-quality black Moors should be sooty black with no bronze overtones.

England first began breeding the animals in 1691. The French became interested in goldfish in the middle of the 18th century when, as legend has it, the Marquise de Pompadour, the mistress of Louis XV, received specimens as a gift. The goldfish's first mention in European text is believed to have been in Billardon de Sauvigny's *Histoire Naturelle des Dorades de la Chine*, a popular volume which furthered the interest in goldfish among the French.

Introduction

The Japanese *Ranchu* Lionhead has no dorsal fin and a chunky body.

Rear Admiral Daniel Ammen brought a large shipment of goldfish to the United States in 1878 which were displayed in Washington, D.C. The Oriental oddities became a sensation and both dealers and private owners began ordering their own shipments of the beautiful aquatic creatures. Maryland was the site of the first established American goldfish farm in 1889.

In World War II the fish were used to identify certain types of poison gas. Today, they have achieved commercial success in many countries, with some hatcheries in the United States reporting an annual production of 5,000,000 fish. American fisheries now lead the world in the production of goldfish.

These commercially produced pet fish are kept in large tanks or outdoor pools. By being kept in properly cleaned surroundings and provided with the correct temperature and diet, they will thrive and often breed several times a year.

Goldfish are extremely pliable genetically, which accounts for the wide variations in the shapes of their bodies,

Pompon Orandas sport exceptional nasal development in addition to their headgrowth.

heads, eyes, fins, and the wide range of colors. However, if left in the wild, they will revert back to their olive-green ancestral color in a very few generations. For the varieties in beauty we have to thank the unknown Chinese breeder who first discovered and separated the natural mutations found in a school of carp. While there are no actual records of the fact, it might be supposed that this ancient Chinese breeder (or a student of his) was also responsible for the fancy varieties of goldfish which were, and are, so popular. The most common of the domestic varieties of goldfish is the Golden Red. Completely white albino varieties (which are blind) were produced by the Chinese, as well as varieties which are white with red fins.

The Japanese developed telescope fish which have short, round bodies, broad heads with protruding eyes and bilobed or trilobed tails. The common telescope goldfish have eyes which are turned outward while the celestal variety have eyes which are turned upwards. The veiltails are a fancy breed characterized by long, veil-like fins. The spotted goldfish of any breed are called the calicoes; fantails are those with two tail fins and two anal fins.

Introduction

Basically, there are two separate types of goldfish, one denoted as "scaled" and the other as "scaleless." Scaleless goldfish possess translucent, nacreous scales in reality, which give them glowing colors such as blues and lavenders. There are also matt goldfish which do not have the "sheen" of their brighter-looking cousins.

Today, pet owners keep their goldfish in aquariums or outdoor ponds. These can be simply or elaborately furnished, keeping the health and welfare of the fish uppermost in mind.

Beautiful, well-cared-for goldfish will be a source of pleasure for years to come.

Goldfish require little attention to their basic needs. Daily care takes no more than a few minutes. The real effort lies in providing the correct environment which includes, among other things, proper water temperature and proper food. Too often people prepare aquariums for exotic beauty and forget that they are creating environments for living creatures. If those environments are not carefully and correctly prepared, you could end up with a beautiful tank of water and nothing else.

Included in the earliest mention of goldfish are references to their royal beauty and wide color varieties. Down through the ages, the genetic variations have been referred to by different common names. Some of these exotic-looking goldfish command high prices from breeders. Goldfish fanciers believe that their beauty is worth the price and populate

VARIETIES OF GOLDFISH

their aquariums or ponds with a multitude of different kinds of swirling and swimming goldfish. Regardless of the type, they all have a common ancestor which, due to the relatively recent intervention of mankind, can be traced with a certain degree of authority.

Every good pet shop owner will do his or her best to offer you a selection of the kinds of goldfish you would like to own. They will also do their best to provide you with healthy fish which will afford you years of pleasure. Nevertheless, it is a good idea for you to learn what to look for in selecting a healthy goldfish.

A healthy goldfish is a happy goldfish. It will be actively swimming, sometimes faster than the eye can follow. The fins should all be in motion as well, guiding the speedy aquatic movements. If the fish you are viewing looks slow and listless and if its dorsal fin is drooping, it is probably sick. If you detect any of these signs, set your heart on a different fish.

The goldfish has its own distinctive series of fins, similar to other fish of the family Cyprinidae. On their backs they have a dorsal fin. Their tail fin is called the caudal fin and, in the Common Goldfish, it is slightly forked. They have pectoral

FACING PAGE:
A goldfish with exceptionally beautiful and delicate finnage is best kept in an aquarium rather than a pond.

fins, one on each side directly behind their gill openings. Behind the pectoral fins, on the underbelly, are the pelvic fins. The anal fin is right behind the goldfish's vent which is approximately midway between the pelvic and anal fins. They have round, clear eyes and nostril openings, one on each side, in front of and slightly above the eyes.

The following contains some descriptions of the goldfish most often encountered by those looking for pets for their aquarium or pond. Most of these varieties can be found in the

Bubble-eyes need to be handled very gently to avoid damage to the delicate eye sacs.

three scale groups: metallic, nacreous and matt. With some goldfish varieties it may be difficult to classify a specific scale group since many exist as combinations of two or all three.

The Common Goldfish looks metallic, its appearance being bright and its scales covering its body in even, imbricated rows. Its coloring can be anything from yellow to orange to red-orange to silver or any blend of these combinations. Some are black, but this coloring will fade, and there are the white albi-

Varieties of Goldfish

In general, the less highly developed and less bizarre-looking goldfish are the hardier.

nos. In some areas the black-marked goldfish are called Orioles. A healthy Common Goldfish has a well-proportioned body with a curved back and underside. The head is wide and short with a small mouth and normal bright eyes. Its moderately sized fins are held stiffly as is its slightly forked tail. The Common Goldfish is a stronger fish than most other varieties, being able to survive in a wider range of temperatures.

In Japan the Wakin is their "common" variety, similar to its western cousin with shorter fins and a double caudal fin.

These magnificent black Orandas are not about to engage in combat. They are unusually inquisitive and friendly.

A variety that is directly developed from the Wakin is the Jikin, looking like a Wakin that has been compressed on a vertical plane. The favorite Jikins are silver with red mouths and fins. The caudal fin appears as an "X" when seen from behind.

The Comet Goldfish is a true American variety, first bred in the ponds of the Washington, D.C. Fish Commission in the late 1880's. Its elongated tail and relatively streamlined body are its prominent features. The fish appeared originally by accident and was later purposely bred. The larger, differently proportioned, deeply forked tail fin makes the Comet Goldfish one of the fastest-swimming varieties. Pet owners who have Comet Goldfish are also cautioned to cover the tops of their aquariums, since Comet Goldfish are known to actually leap from the tank during their faster-than-the-eye-can-follow swimming and darting. The Comet Goldfish is usually yellow in color, but most fish enthusiasts seek red-orange coloring.

The Japanese Fantail moves much more slowly than its Comet cousin but both share common ancestry. They appear with both single and double tail and anal fins, the doubles being more popular among serious fish fanciers.

The ancestors of the spectacular fancy goldfish were probably very similar to this humble-looking cyprinid fish.

Varieties of Goldfish

This bronze Oranda has considerably less headgrowth and can see better than some of its cousins.

The Veiltail Goldfish are seen with either normal or telescope eyes. They have deep, round bodies, deeper than they are long. They have a long, broad, gracefully folded caudal with a squared lower edge which is divided into two identical fins. This parallel division is also evident in their anal fin. These beautiful features do not fully develop until the fish is in its second year of life and will continue to grow if the fish is overfed. If this is the case, the edges of these graceful fins may become ragged and split. The ideal proportions of the Veiltail Goldfish's fins call for the dorsal fin to be as wide as the fish's body with the tail fin being twice the body length. Experts recommend that the food intake be reduced at this stage of development so the beauty of this finnage will be maintained. The Veiltail is also known as the Fringetail, Gauzetail, Lacetail, Muslintail and Ribbontail Goldfish. Veiltail Goldfish with single anal and tail fins are often called Nymphs.

The Shubunkin looks like the Common Goldfish, but its coloring is normally in patches of black, brown, blue, lavender or red on a pearl or light blue background color. Bright red Shubunkins with black spots are common with full purple or laven-

der ones being rarer. The Shubunkins are scaleless, a result of breeding a Common Goldfish with a Demekin. Another variety, called the London Shubunkin, is identical to the Common Goldfish except that it has transparent scales having no metallic look. They are seen in solid colors and white. Among experts the most valued ones have a bright blue background color with patches of black, red, violet and brown and a flecked pattern of black. These colors cover the fish and extend to its fins. In certain areas of the world, the Shubunkin is known as the Vermilion Variegated Goldfish and the Speckled or Harlequin Goldfish.

This calico Bristol Shubunkin is streamlined with long, well-developed fins.

The Bristol Shubunkin is streamlined, having a depth that is less than half the fish's body length and a small head. Its fins are long and well-developed, especially the caudal fin.

A Demekin is a pop-eyed fish most often found with black scales (often called Kuro Demekin) turning light red or light orange (Aka Demekin) as the fish gets older. The black of these fish is due to an unusual amount of the metallic pigment. The iridescent-looking variety is referred to as Sanshoko De-

The deep red coloration of this white and red *Ryukin* is controlled by sunlight and color-enhancing food.

mekin. The body shape of these fish resembles the Ryukin Goldfish.

Ryukin is a short, narrow variety with a hump where its head meets its body. After the Wakin, it is the most popular Japanese goldfish. It has longer fins than the Wakin and a forked caudal which is divided into two fins. It also has a pair of anal fins. In western regions a version of the Ryukin is known as the Fantail which is seen in both telescope and normal configurations. It has no pronounced hump and the fins are somewhat shorter and paddle shaped. The most prized of the Fantails are the Red Metallics, known for being very hardy fish.

The Pearlscale is normally a silver-colored fish distinguished by large red patches. It has a flat back, fat body and a pointed, small-mouthed head. Its fins are similar to those of the Fantail variety of Ryukin with its divided caudal fin not as deeply forked. The name is derived from its dome-shaped scales with the outer edges of each individual scale being darker than the raised center. When reflecting light, the fish looks like it is covered with tiny pearls. If a scale is lost, oddly enough, it will be replaced by an ordinary one.

The Tosakin also appears to have come from the Ryu-kin, but it has a body which looks shallower. The lower lobes of its caudal fin are turned up at the edges and are more extended than those of the Ryukin. This gives the appearance that the fin has been reversed, making it difficult for the fish to swim. Since they cannot spawn naturally, they must be stripped by hand and should only be kept in an aquarium and never in a pool.

Calico Telescope Goldfish are short and squat, which is a genetic characteristic of all telescope varieties, as are their

The calico Telescope Goldfish are excellent companions for the limited-vision bubble-eyes.

pop-eyes. They have a mottled color like the Shubunkin and are one of the most popular varieties. The two scaleless Chinese goldfish types are the Calico Fantail, distinguished by the absence of the telescope eyes, and the Plain Scaleless, some of which have the pop-eyes, some of which do not. They can be red, white or a mottled coloring of red and white. Both of these latter types are extremely translucent, allowing the eggs of the female to actually be visible when the fish swims in front of a light source.

Varieties of Goldfish

Telescope Goldfish are those fish which have protruding eyes. They are also called Pop-eyed Goldfish by some and Dragon Eyes by the Chinese. However, since the unusual eye development sometimes does not appear until the fish is two months to two years old, the fish are also known under specific classifications. These protruding eyes will continue to develop for as long as the fish lives. Opposite of what might be presumed, the larger the protrusion of the eye, the more myopic the fish appear to be.

The Moors are small goldfish with a smooth, velvet, soot-like coloring. They are also seen in light red and light orange colors. They have telescope eyes and have fins identical to the Veiltails. A well-developed Moor is considered the pinnacle of goldfish breeding in Britain. They are very similar to the Japanese Demekin, some experts citing them as the same variety. They are also referred to as the Blackamoor. They are not the

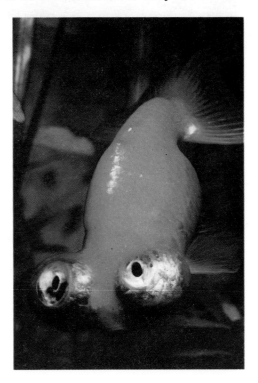

If the fish is mishandled, the eyes of the Telescope Goldfish may literally fall off!

hardiest of goldfish and should not be quartered in ponds except in the warmer summer months where the water is at least 65 degrees.

The name Celestial Goldfish is derived from the fact that the pupils of its protruding eyes are always on top of the eyeball, pointing upwards, i.e. heavenward. It has also been called The Sky-Gazer, Star-Gazer or the Heavenward Dragon. Their bodies resemble the Chinese Telescope or Ryukin varieties and they are black or light orange in color. They do not swim well, preferring to rest on their bellies at the bottom of the aquarium. Their eyes cause a disadvantage when feeding them with other varieties since they have difficulty seeing live food. It is recommended that Celestials be kept in an aquarium (not a pool) populated with other Celestials.

Toadhead Goldfish look like Celestials with normal eyes and a bladder-like growth that makes their heads look like toads.

The Lionhead Goldfish has no dorsal fin, a globe-shaped body and a humped back which makes it a poor swimmer. It is often observed swimming upside down or vertically in order to maintain the balance of its awkward body. The odd growth of the Lionhead's head (also called in some quarters a Buffalohead or Hooded Goldfish) normally develops by the beginning of the second year, continuing to grow afterwards. Sometimes this growth will cover the fish's gill plates and it will die of suffocation even under ideal conditions. They are usually colored like the Common Goldfish, with smokey-colored bodies and yellow heads not being uncommon. There are subdivisions of Lionheads in Japan, each named after the breeders who developed them. They are called Ranchu in Japan and the most popular varieties have very high, arched caudal fins, deep, round bodies with broad backs and short fins. They, like all Lionheads, lack the dorsal fin, but have double caudal fins and paired anal fins. The Osaka Ranchu has a small, pointed head which does not grow and a double, fan-like caudal fin. The Edonishiki is identical to the Ranchu except for the color variations and the head growth is not considered as good. The Nankin Ranchu has a somewhat longer body, no head growth, and a silver body with red-tipped mouth and fins. The Chinese Lion-

heads are identical to the American or Japanese varieties but they have larger hoods and fins.

The Pompon has the Lionhead's body and fins, but the head appears normal. There are two types of Pompons, one with a dorsal fin, one without. The narial septa, the flesh that divides the Pompon's nostrils, are enlarged into what are known as narial bouquets. These enlarged lobes of flesh are often sucked in and out of the fish's mouth. This is where this classification of goldfish gets its name since these lobes look like the pompons on hats or costumes.

The Phoenix is of Chinese origin and looks like an equal cross between a Ranchu and a Common Goldfish without a dorsal fin. It has very long fins, a pair of anal fins and a deeply forked double caudal fin.

The Oranda Goldfish are considered modifications of the Lionhead, having similar coloring but shaped more along the lines of a Veiltail, possessing a dorsal fin. The head growth of the Oranda does not come down over the gills; it is confined to the top of the head. Nevertheless, this variety is considered fragile and should be kept in an aquarium rather than a pond. Color variations of the Oranda are sometimes identified under separate classifications such as the Azumanishiki and Redcap

Tetuonaga or black *Ryukin*.

Oranda. This latter classification refers to the red growths on the fish's head resembling warts. There is also a variety known for the same reasons as the Redcap.

Other types include the Bubble-eye which has fluid-filled bladders below their otherwise normal eyes, and Meteor, which has an egg-shaped body and lacks a caudal fin because of over-development of the other finnage.

Some goldfish cannot compete for food and tank space and should be kept only with other goldfish that are similar in size and make-up.

Varieties of Goldfish

Experts estimate that there are probably **125 or more** varieties of fancy goldfish, including types we did not detail such as the Maruko (the Japanese Egg-Fish), the Blue Fish (known in China as the Lan-yu) and the Watonai (a cross between the Common Goldfish and the Veiltail). With the ever-increasing number of amateur and professional goldfish breeders, new variations will, no doubt, continue to be bred. It is important to remember that the nature of selective breeding produces weaker varieties while it causes more exotic and beautiful

If a bubble-eye's sac should inadvertently burst and the injury is not severe, it will usually regenerate in time.

ones. The more removed a variety is from its original ancestor, the less hardy it becomes. This is why many of the rarer goldfish are not seen all around the world. Their frailty prevents long travels even though the transporting of fish has become more and more sophisticated. This is also the reason that you must consult your pet store owner when originally acquiring your fish as to whether or not they will be able to survive better in an aquarium or in an outdoor pond.

AQUARIUMS & POOLS

Many people who are seriously considering taking on the responsibility of caring for goldfish sometimes balk at the idea because of expense. They have seen the beautiful but elaborate aquariums and pools at their local pet shop and are dissuaded because of what they imagine to be an extravagance. In reality, if set up properly an outdoor pool or aquarium can be a thing of beauty for a relatively small amount of money. Of course careful shopping will help, but there are other considerations before committing time, money and effort to housing your pet goldfish.

The first decision that must be made is whether to keep your goldfish in an aquarium or an outdoor pool. Since pools need more preparation and planning, we will initially concentrate on the aquarium, which can be an attractive and often exotic addition to any home.

Having an indoor aquarium provides a better opportunity to view the mysterious splendor of your swimming and darting goldfish. With a glass aquarium, you will be able to see your fish from the top and sides and they will not be able to hide on the bottom. Also, the normal arrangement of an aquarium gives you a perfect view of your goldfish's world so you can be on the early alert for any problems that may arise.

Some of the disadvantages of keeping your goldfish indoors include the fact that their colors will not be as bright and there will be less natural food of the variety that normally fall into an outside pool. Goldfish kept indoors also do not experience seasonal changes to the same degree as their outdoor

FACING PAGE:
The headgrowth is highly prized
among goldfish hobbyists.

A power head filter attachment will help keep your aquarium very well aerated and will provide good water movement.

counterparts. Outside fish tend to become hardier because of their exposure and resulting natural resistance to harsher temperature changes.

The two big drawbacks of an aquarium environment for the novice goldfish keeper are overcrowding and overfeeding. Since there is limited space, it does not take much uneaten food to pollute the water.

The best size aquarium for a beginner would be about a 20 to 30 gallon capacity. These come in various styles and shapes. Rectangular all-glass aquariums with flat sides and sometimes with plastic upper frames are considered best. These are readily available at your local pet store. All-glass aquariums are very reasonably priced. Depending on the amount of money you wish to spend, some pet shops can make custom tanks to fit the decor of your home.

Since aquariums need aeration to support the fish living within, the greater the area of water exposed directly to the air, the more fish you can have in your aquarium. This is why

a shallow and wide aquarium is better than a deep and narrow one. The surface of the water is greater, allowing more gaseous exchange. Even if two aquariums hold equal amounts of water, a shallow and wide one will be able to support more fish.

This rule also applies to goldfish bowls. The shapes of these bowls are normally very narrow at the top. If you choose a standard goldfish bowl, fill it only to where the water level is at the *widest* part of the bowl. A good rule of thumb for determining the capacity of your aquarium is that there should be 20 square inches of water surface for every inch of fish, measured from the mouth to the end of the body (not including the tail fins). With this formula in mind, overcrowding should not be a problem.

Speaking of goldfish bowls, we must point out here that fish experts do not recommend the use of bowls for goldfish. They cite the small bowls as the reason behind quick deaths of many children's pet goldfish since the containers are generally too small for the fish. They give the faster swimming varieties no room to dart around, making them more prisoners rather than pets to be viewed and admired. The water is quickly soiled in such small containers and, as some devoted fanciers complain, the very shapes of goldfish bowls distort the exotic beauty of the fish.

After acquiring an aquarium, the first thing you should do is fill it with water and check it for leaks. Aquariums are fragile and sometimes the slightest jarring will break the seals, causing a leak.

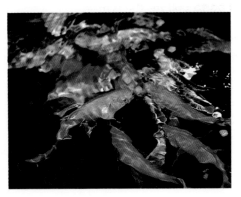

Goldfish are eager eaters, especially when there's competition.

If a leak is a slow and minor one, empty the tank and seal the cracks in the seams with silicone cement available at your pet shop. Fill it and check for leaks once again. Some people have tried to seal a tank while it is still full by applying sealants to the outside. The water pressure from the inside of the tank, no matter how slight, is greater than the air pressure outside. Eventually, the water will break an outside seal. If you al-

Flowers edging a pond are lovely and natural. Avoid building a pond near trees, however; fallen leaves may pollute your water.

ways repair a tank on the inside, the water pressure will aid in keeping the seal tight.

Some novice fish keepers may suppose that cleanliness is not all that important since many fish thrive in some of the world's most polluted waters. One difference is that these outside locations of the wild are exposed to the open air. While air and water pollution may be extreme in many areas, this outside

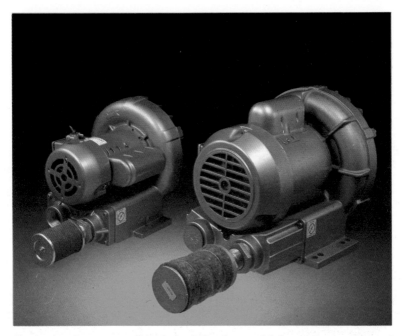

Garden ponds are aerated with the help of powerful heavy-duty pumps and compressors.

environment allows a certain amount of natural recycling of water through evaporation and regular rainfall. In the confined conditions of your aquarium, no such natural cleaning takes place. Your goldfish need some applied effort on your part.

Your next consideration should be where to place your aquarium. Actually, this should be planned carefully *before* you even decide to bring goldfish into your home. If you place it where it will receive strong sunlight, you'll quickly lose sight of all your fish. Direct sunlight on the sides of your aquarium will generate the growth of algae (microscopic plants). These will form a film which will cloud the sides in a remarkably short time. Unfortunately, prolonged periods out of sunlight will cause the necessary aquarium plants to die. The ideal location should be a place where the tank receives about an hour's worth of natural sunlight per day. The plants will thrive and the algae growth will be slowed. The algae is a natural and healthy occurrence within the tank, since these tiny plants help to purify the water and sand in the tank by digesting a portion of floating waste material. Many fanciers suggest scraping the film off the front of the tank and letting it remain on the back and

Goldfish raised in outdoor ponds can achieve incredible size and color due to sunlight, spacious quarters, and an abundance of natural foods.

sides. Many fanciers find the algae growth on ornamental aquarium rocks very attractive. However, algae growth which appears hairy or filamentous should be removed as soon as possible after it is detected.

If an ideal location providing an hour's daily sunlight cannot be found in your home, there is no need to give up the idea of having an aquarium for your goldfish. You will have probably noticed that your local pet shop dealer illuminates his tanks with artificial lighting. Such lighting is needed if natural lighting is unavailable and if you want to be able to show off

Many people further enhance the beauty of their fish ponds with water lilies and lotus plants.

your goldfish at night. If this is what you desire, a metal reflector will be needed. In the majority of cases, such reflectors are included with a new aquarium. They normally feature all the needed electrical sockets and a fluorescent light bulb. The reflectors with the fluorescent bulbs are the most popular since they give off less heat. Incandescent lights will actually increase the water temperature as much as 10 degrees. If you use too powerful an incandescent bulb, the heat generated will probably increase the algae growth on the tank's glass and decorations. Also, if you shut off such lights or if there is a sudden power failure, the radical water temperature drop could be a shock to

your goldfish. With automatic air conditioning in most modern homes, this problem does not arise too often, but it should still be an important consideration.

If you want illumination even if your tank receives adequate natural daylight, maintain a relatively low wattage so the temperature change of the water will not be so sudden and radical. This is especially important during the cooler months, but can be controlled easily by the installation of an aquarium heater and thermostat. Heaters for goldfish are not as necessary as they are for tropical fish, which are affected more by drastic temperature changes and have to live in a more limited temperature range. Keeping your aquarium on the cool side during cooler winter months will prevent the goldfish from becoming sluggish and they will be more vigorous in the spring. A wide variety of heaters are also available at your local pet store. Tailor the heater you choose to the size of your tank. Also, make sure the room in which you place your aquarium is relatively dust-free, and that it has not been freshly painted. Dust, tobacco and paint fumes are especially harmful to goldfish. Your aquarium can be protected by placing a pane of glass over the top about ¼ inch from the surface of the water so that air may freely circulate.

The bottom of your tank should be covered with gravel in which the necessary aquarium plants will be able to grow and thrive. A good rule of thumb to follow for gravel is 20 pounds for every ten gallons of water. Choose a grade of gravel with ⅛ inch particles since finer varieties will become saturated and packed down and coarser types will form crevices in which uneaten food can become trapped and eventually pollute the water in the tank.

The gravel should be cleaned before introducing it into your tanks. There are commercially cleaned varieties available at your pet store, but all of these require additional cleaning before use. Place the gravel in a bucket or pail and, using a warm flow of water, stir it continually until the water which runs off appears clean and free of sediment. Since the bottoms of natural rivers and ponds do not have an even layer of sand or gravel, neither should your aquarium. You can aid in the natural look by adding smooth slate stones to the bottom. Slate is a good choice since it will not dissolve like limestone or sandstone might, changing the chemical balance of the water. Aquarium stones, both real and artificial, must be smooth to keep your fish safe from accidental injury.

After you have added the gravel and plants to the tank, you are ready to fill it with water. One easy way to do this without disturbing your decor is to place a bowl on the bottom of the tank and direct a gentle stream of water into the bowl. Aging your water is important to the future health of your fish. You can either let the water in the aquarium sit for a few days before adding fish or purchase one of the commercial chlorine removers available at your pet shop.

Vacuuming devices are indispensable for keeping goldfish in aquaria.

Sunlight really brings
out goldfish's colors!

Ducks love to eat small
fishes. Even frogs and turtles are
trouble for pond fish.

Filters for aquariums come in many different varieties and help to maintain the crystal clarity of the water. They operate by cycling the water through a chamber of charcoal and other filtering agents with the aid of a quiet motor. Clearing the water is the major function of such an apparatus. One popular variety is the undergravel filter which is placed in the bottom of the aquarium prior to laying down the sand or gravel bed.

Other devices include an aerator which continually

pumps bubbles of air into the tank's water, helping to remove carbon dioxide gas dissolved in the water. You will probably see quite a few of these in operation at your local pet store.

While plants help to create more beautiful natural settings, this is not their main purpose. They help to purify the water and gravel; certain types give your goldfish added nourishment and they provide hiding places for your goldfish and their eggs. They can also be arranged in such a way as to hide filters or water heaters.

If your aquarium plants are to perform as they should, they first need a good root system, which a proper gravel-covered bottom should provide.

Your local pet store owner will probably be able to advise you on exactly the right balance of plants. Before you plant any of them, make sure all the dead branches and leaves are removed and that they are completely free of any clinging insects. One way to insure this is to purchase a plant sterilizing solution at your pet shop.

Many man-made ponds look very natural.

Many goldfish experts frown on adding ornaments to their aquariums, feeling that the beauty of the plants and the fish themselves are enough. However, they recognize that ornaments are a matter of individual preference. It is best to remember when adding such things to your aquarium to stick strictly to those types which were specifically designed for aquarium use and that have no sharp edges where the fish could injure themselves. A wide variety of these are available at your pet store.

Cleaning your aquarium is not a difficult operation, especially in a simple, basic setup. When the setting becomes unsightly with mulm, dirt, etc., use a 5-foot siphon tube to siphon off the dirt into a bucket. Using water of a temperature equal to that in the tank, replace the amount of removed water. Goldfish can survive in temperatures between just above freezing to approximately 85°F but seem to prefer temperature between 65° and 70°F. They also do not like any sudden temperature fluctuation. Be careful that no goldfish swim too near the end

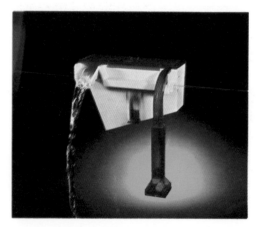

A power filter will help keep the water in your aquarium crystal clear and sparkling.

of the siphoning tube since they can be harmed by the suction force, especially those fish with protruding eyes.

There are also a number of scavengers you can add to the natural environment of your goldfish. Your local pet shop owner will be able to suggest the proper varieties of snails, mussels, salamanders, tadpoles, weatherfish, etc. to introduce

The corner filter is attached to an air pump and purifies water through floss and charcoal.

to your aquarium to help keep it clean. These animals will eat excess algae, uneaten food and even expired fish that may have sunk undetected to the bottom.

Goldfish are able to tolerate just about any kind of water: soft, hard, alkaline, acidic, etc. In outdoor ponds their growth is more rapid and their colors are brighter, but otherwise, they do well in normal aquarium water conditions. Some experts note that delicate varieties such as Veiltails appear to need soft water with neutral pH and that **no** goldfish will live in absolutely soft water such as distilled water or rainwater. Since some tap water is chlorinated, and too much chlorination can be harmful to goldfish, many fish fanciers recommend adding chlorine remover to any new water added to your tank. Your local pet store will have supplies of this for quick removal of chlorine. Remember that chlorinated water exposed to the air for two or three days will become completely safe since the chlorine will be neutralized. Also, if you heat the water to 180°F for about 30 minutes, the chlorine will be removed and make the water completely safe to use as soon as the temperature drops down to match the existing water temperature the goldfish like.

The recommended way to introduce your pet goldfish into its new home when you bring it from the store is to do so gradually. In nature, all changes are gradual, especially in temperature. Even if there is a sudden drop in the overall temperature, water temperature changes slowly. For this reason, pet

This pond, which could be anywhere in Japan, is actually in the United States.

shop owners should place your new fish in a plastic bag in water from its original tank. After you bring the fish home, float the bag in the aquarium for about 20 minutes, allowing the water temperatures to equalize. Then open the bag, allowing the water to mix and the fish to swim free. This will do much to prevent any shock to the goldfish caused by radical environmental changes.

*   *   *

A natural setting for goldfish is an outdoor pool or ornamental pond. Proper location of such a pond is very important. Remember that plants are necessary in the environment of your goldfish and plants need sunlight, no matter how hardy they are. It is fairly easy to construct some kind of artificial shading for a pond that is in direct sunlight, but very difficult to introduce light in a perpetually shaded pond. You must also make certain your proposed site is not in a place where too many leaves will be dropping into the water. These will eventually decompose and pollute your goldfish's home to such a degree as to be harmful or even fatal. Check the varieties of plants and

trees surrounding the area where you plan to construct your pool. Certain types of plants and trees have leaves which contain substances toxic to your fish. Your local pet shop owner will be able to advise you on the varieties you should avoid.

Many goldfish fanciers prefer an informal-shaped pool with a low wall for sitting and viewing as well as protecting children from accidental falls into the pool. They may be constructed from various materials including pre-formed vinyl, concrete blocks, reinforced concrete, bricks or fiberglass; or miniature pools can be made from kettles, tanks or tubs.

Many pet store owners can advise you as to the proper way to actually install your pool if you want to do it yourself. There are also any number of good books that will help you make the right decisions about the construction and site of

Fish in ponds can become very tame and eagerly anticipate feeding time.

your pond. If you don't wish to tackle such a job yourself, there are local contractors who specialize in ornamental pool construction with widely varying price ranges depending on the location, size, and style. If you have someone put such a pool in for you, remember the importance of their paying close attention to the needs of the fish which will inhabit the finished product. As is the case with aquariums, the goldfish and their overall welfare should be your initial and primary concern.

For more detailed information about pond construction and management, consult the specialized books available in pet shops.

FEEDING

Aquarium goldfish are very active in every season of the year. They should be fed at least once a day, twice if they are good eaters. Pond goldfish need to be well fed twice a day during the warmer months since they hibernate in cold weather and do not eat during these times of the year. If they do eat they will not be able to properly digest their food. They live off their own body fat during their long inactive periods.

There may be an abundance of natural food available to pond goldfish because of earthworms being attracted to the water, gnat and midge eggs, etc., but there is rarely enough of this type of nourishment to properly produce the needed winter energy. The fish will eat almost constantly if this type of natural food is present, but they will still need supplementary food from their owner.

Always feed your fish at regular intervals, even if they appear to be searching for food at other times during the day.

One of the greatest causes of early death in aquarium goldfish is overfeeding. Although generally considered omnivorous, it must always be remembered that, being members of the carp family, goldfish are mostly vegetable eaters and they eat off the bottom of the aquarium. Most experts agree that it is better to feed your aquarium fish many small meals at frequent intervals than one large meal. The more familiar you are with the varieties of food available, the better.

Goldfish, like most animals, require foods from different groups for healthy survival. They need varying amounts of vitamins, minerals, protein, fat and carbohydrates. Vitamins such as A (which gives the goldfish its healthy coloring), D, E, K,   B6 and C are all necessary to a good goldfish diet. Vita-

FACING PAGE:
An orange Chinese Lionhead. Note the lack of dorsal fin.

min A can be found in the dark green freshwater algae that form in the aquarium. It is also present in egg yolks and pink shrimp shells.

Most of the commercially available goldfish foods contain the necessary amounts of the required minerals goldfish need. Some of these include iron, zinc, copper, cobalt and iodine.

Amino acids make up the proteins which the goldfish need for the formation of tissue.. Goldfish food should contain at least 12% protein. Goldfish need fats for energy but too much fat (over 4%) will cause fatty degeneration of the liver and should be avoided.

Carbohydrates are found in the sugars and starches of the goldfish diet. These are present in the plants you will observe the goldfish nipping upon in their aquariums and pools.

There are many varieties of prepared commercial goldfish food. There are dried and frozen varieties, different live foods and even scraps from your table that your goldfish will enjoy and thrive upon. It is best to stick to using the types of

While goldfish are not fussy eaters, good quality foods fed in a wide variety will keep them in prime condition.

There are many types of food. Just don't overfeed.

food that are generally acceptable by the experts in the field. These include such things as ant pupae, aphids, *asellus*, bloodworms, cyclops, *daphnia*, earthworms, *gammarus*, glassworms, grindal worms, maggots, microworms, micro-eels, mosquito larvae, rat-tailed maggots, tadpoles, tubifex, and whiteworms.

In all cases of live food, consult with your local pet store as to the specifics of finding and cultivating these edible creatures. Many of the varieties mentioned do not actually have to be hunted out in nearby swamps, but are readily available in your pet store. If a certain variety is not available, your pet store operator might know of a fish fancier who does hunt up his own live food supply. You can be placed in direct contact with this person through your store and an arrangement for fresh live food might be able to be made.

Naturally, your pet store is the place for all commercial pet foods which have become, in recent years, abundant. They are available in freeze dried, fresh frozen and dried preparations. They all come with detailed instructions for proper feeding. Your individual circumstances will determine feeding time and frequencies. Your pet store owner will be able to guide you along these lines as well.

We stress this warning: Remember that one of the two major causes for the early death of goldfish is overfeeding.

BREEDING

If you want to breed your own pet goldfish, you can do so right in your aquarium or pond provided the area is large enough, being not less than 30 inches long. If this is your plan, be sure that the very center of the tank or pool is clear of plants, while each end is well planted. Your pet store owner can tell you which specific plants should be present for breeding purposes in either an aquarium or a goldfish pond.

Preparing your goldfish for breeding is largely a matter of diet. Using temperature as your guide rather than the time of year, you should feed your fish steadily on garden worms. Some experts recommend feeding the fish pair or trio a cup of *Chironomus* larvae (common bloodworms). They have reported success with a single feeding, but, in most cases, multiple feedings of this diet are needed to stimulate spawning. With the artificial light and heat of an aquarium, it is possible to have broods hatch year 'round. However, springtime, with the higher temperatures is usually the best time to spawn goldfish. If the temperature is raised anywhere from five to ten degrees, either naturally or artificially, goldfish can usually be stimulated. If the water temperature is already at 65 degrees or higher, lowering it by 5 degrees has a similar effect. In all cases of trying different temperature changes, the health of the goldfish should still remain the primary concern.

Since the odds of having at least two male/female pairs in any selection of six young goldfish are good, most experts recommend buying six youngsters instead of selecting any sort of mating trio consisting of two males and a female, as some people opt for. During the breeding season, females appear stouter on one side.

FACING PAGE:
Goldfish are very malleable genetically, which has
resulted in over 125 different types.

Determining the sex of goldfish is relatively easy during the breeding season each spring. Raised tubercles about the size of a pinhead appear on the gill-plate of the male and on the leading rays of the pectoral fins. These are sometimes referred to as pearl organs. These pearl organs excite the females during the pre-spawning chase. The tubercles disappear soon after spawning. During the same period the females, especially the more slender varieties, are stouter on one side indicating the presence of ova. In rare instances, some female goldfish develop tubercles and some males do not.

Another method that is not always 100% accurate is selecting as male those fish who initiate a pre-spawning chase.

Healthy, well-fed goldfish will spawn more readily, and the quality of the eggs will be better.

This chase is why the plants are needed at each end of your aquarium and why you must be certain that all rocks with uneven edges are removed. If your goldfish are in a pond, make certain that all rough edges are covered with plants so the fish will not be injured during the pre-spawning chase.

This rather unenthusiastic chase will cause the female to dart around until she realizes that contact with some of your

Breeding

After the spawning chase the female will hide in the plants and discharge her tiny eggs.

plants and the subsequent struggle will relieve her of ripe ova. If there are no males present, the females may begin such chases to relieve themselves. Sometimes such a chase can be witnessed by an entire school of males as well.

After the chase, the female will hide in a convenient clump of growth and, by means of a rapid and violent flapping motion, will spray her eggs while the male sometimes presses his gill-plates against her head or abdomen. The eggs are minute, some smaller than a grain of sugar. They are very absorbent however, and will often double in size as soon as they are sprayed and begin absorbing water. The eggs must be fertilized before or during the intake of this water or they will not survive.

A micropyle, a small opening in each egg, absorbs the male's sperm that is given off when he sheds his reproductive secretion, called milt. There is no actual contact between the sexes for fertilization of the eggs.

Active males will single out a female and drive her vigorously through the water. As spawning draws closer, the drive becomes more prolonged and violent.

The eggs are demersal adhesive, which means they are coated with a sticky organic substance and are heavier than water. This characteristic causes the eggs to sink to the bottom of the pool or aquarium and become fastened to whatever they touch as they sink to the lower regions of the water.

Since fish will often eat their own eggs, there should be provisions made for a separate container for the aquatic plants on which the fertilized eggs adhere. A separate aquarium or even a shallow pan will be adequate as long as it has a sufficient surface area and allows the plant enough light and air. If the plant begins to die or decay the resulting rot may foul and pollute the water, endangering both plant and eggs. You should keep the temperature of this water anywhere between 70–75°F. The eggs should hatch in about four days. The amount of time the eggs take to develop is completely in relation to water temperature. If you keep the water warmer than these recommended temperatures, the eggs could hatch within 2½ or 3 days. Lower temperatures could delay the hatching for as much as two weeks. This extended period can be dangerous since there is more time and opportunity for the fragile ova to be damaged or destroyed.

It is unlikely that all of the fry will hatch at the same time or even on the same day. They usually emerge over a two to three day span. Since growth is rapid during these initial stages, the fry that hatch earlier are quite a bit larger than those that hatch late. These larger specimens will often eat the smaller ones during the initial weeks of life. It will be necessary to separate the larger ones to prevent this from happening.

When newly hatched, the fry have not, as yet, developed normal mouths and have, instead, suckers which allow them to hang on the smooth glass sides of aquariums. They live off the remains of the yolk sac on their ventral surface for the first two or three days. Once the contents of the yolk sac are

After the female has laid the eggs, the male fertilizes them with "milt."

absorbed, they release themselves and go in search of food. There are a number of creatures (besides the parents) which devour newly hatched fry, such as hydra and snails, but these should not be a problem if you have moved the fry to a safe breeding tank prior to hatching. Your plants will have been properly prepared so none of these pests will remain hiding on any of them.

There are many excellent diets that may be given newly hatched goldfish fry, but the most popular one appears to be a natural microscopic lifeform called infusoria. Since an average spawn numbers anywhere from 500 to 1,000, they will

need quite a large amount of food for their first two weeks of life. This must be prepared in advance so you will have enough on hand to feed them from the very beginning. You will need quart-sized mason jars to which you have added lettuce or hay heated just to the point of boiling. Fill each jar with water and wait for about three days. In that time, protozoans known as *Paramecium* will have developed in the thousands.

Once you see the fry begin their food search, pour a jar of your *Paramecium* into the tank, all except for the hay or

Immediately after spawning, remove either the eggs or the parents, as goldfish are notorious egg-eaters.

lettuce piece and a small amount of the water. Using old aquarium water, refill the jar right away and new *Paramecium* will begin development immediately and be ready in another couple of days. Do not store the jars in direct sunlight. Temperatures of 100°F will destroy them. There are a number of commercially available fry foods at your local pet store. If you do not want to go through the trouble of developing your own *Paramecium*, there are modern infusoria pills that make producing the cultures very easy.

In approximately two weeks, the fry will have devel-

The Shubunkin is a very hardy single-tailed fish and was first developed in Japan in the early 1900's by Mr. Kichigoro Akiyama.

oped enough to demand a larger and more complex diet. *Daphnia pulex*, a small fresh water crustacean, develops in still or stagnant water and, when the quantity is great enough, causes the water to appear red. They are an excellent source of food for two-week-old goldfish fry, but they are too large for the minute goldfish to digest. However, since *Daphnia* are continually producing offspring, you can take a small handful of them and strain them through coarse muslin and the *Daphnia* larva that are sifted through will be perfect for the fry. These are called *nauplii* and they are also available commercially. *Artemia salina* (or Brine Shrimp) are also good for newly hatched goldfish young as are mosquito rafts. This latter variety is quite difficult to maintain properly because of their rapid growth. Advice from your pet store owner or other goldfish expert would be advisable if you wish to experiment with raising this variety of live food.

Artificial foods, in the opinion of many experts, seldom produce satisfactory results since many varieties contain large amounts of powdered egg yolks, etc. Much of this material often goes uneaten and appears at the bottom as a reddish patch.

This little fellow is ninety-six hours old. Soon he will wriggle free and start his lifelong search for food.

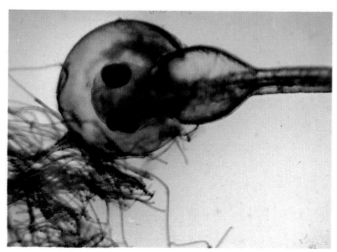

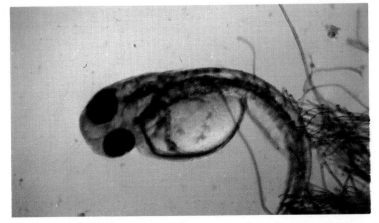

The newly hatched fry is ready to embark on life. The bulbous area is the yolk sac, which will be absorbed in a few days.

This can quickly pollute your aquarium water and goldfish fry are especially susceptible to the dangers of polluted water. When the fry are free-swimming it is safe to introduce snails into the aquarium to aid in the clearing up of such resulting pollution.

These early weeks are also the time when gill flukes or *Gyrodactyliasis* may show up in the new hatchlings. This condition is caused by the presence of the parasite known as *Gyrodactylus elegans*. If you notice that any of the fry are remaining on the surface of the water, this is probably the cause since *Gyrodactyliasis* affects breathing and makes it difficult. Closer examination of fry that are suspected of suffering from *Gyrodactyliasis* will show that they appear to have a tiny white beard. Unfortunately, it is necessary to destroy any fish that are attacked by such parasites so early in their lives. Also, you will have to carefully remove the remainder of the healthy fry to a clean tank filled with aged aquarium water that has already been prepared at the same temperature as the water from which they are being removed. To further combat the presence of this problem, be sure to continue a good diet of live food.

GOLDFISH HEALTH

Most varieties of goldfish are very hardy, so the instances of disease and death are few. This may sound very contrary to the novice goldfish keeper who probably had some of the tiny fish years ago and remembers them living for an extremely short amount of time. Since most of these pets belonging to children were kept either in too little water or too small a space and were very often overfed, the frequent mortality rate is not surprising. With a little knowledge, however, you will find that you will be able to enjoy your goldfish for many years.

Goldfish kept in too little water die, most often, because their water is polluted. The dangers of polluted water exist in the best kept aquariums and pools as well since it is under such conditions that bacterial diseases breed. Polluted water is almost always the initial cause of bacterial diseases in goldfish. The best preventive for such diseases is for your tank or pool to be thoroughly disinfected at the outset. If pollution arises after your pool or aquarium has already been established, there is a combination of steps you can take. First of all, if the pollution is caused by uneaten food, reduce the amount of food at each mealtime. You can also introduce additional plant life to your fish's environment, the presence of which will help to combat the pollution.

You must attend to any afflicted fish as soon as possible. Sickness and infection can spread rapidly in the aquatic environment. It is probably wise to keep medical supplies for your fish well-stocked and handy. Your pet shop owner will be able

FACING PAGE:
A Bubble-eye's sacs make it impossible for the fish to look down and therefore severely restrict its vision.

to advise you on the kinds of remedies you should keep on hand in case you face a medical emergency for your fish.

Speaking of your pet store owner, he or she is the best person to consult if you suspect that any disease or infection is plaguing your pool or aquarium. Realizing that most goldfish illness is the direct result of neglect or ignorance on the part of the owner, the best preventive measure is a little bit of knowledge.

Goldfish are very sensitive to anything out of the ordinary. If it is necessary to handle them use a fine mesh net instead of your hands. This reduces the chance of damaging the fish's scales or fins. If you *must* handle the fish, be sure your hands are wet. When using a net, don't chase the fish with it. Submerge it in the water and let the fish swim around it a bit to become used to its presence. Eventually it will swim inside and you will be able to scoop it up. Do so slowly and, when placing it back in water, submerge the net again and let the fish swim out on its own. Never dump the fish from the net back into the water. Rough handling of this sort could cause your fish to go into a state of nervous shock. This condition is more common in female fish than in males and often is caused by too hard a spawning drive, the chase prior to the laying of eggs.

If your fish suffers from nervous shock (for whatever reason) it should be put in a separate tank in a quiet spot away from any outside activity. Complete rest is the remedy for this condition. Don't approach this isolation tank unless you must and then do so quietly and slowly. Before placing your afflicted fish in this "rest home," you should stir in ¼ ounce of Epsom salts to every gallon of water. Hold off feeding the fish for two days and then begin a diet of chopped earthworms. Continue this until the fish demonstrates its normal, calm activities.

Any change in the general behavior of your fish may be a sign of illness. If they begin to swim unbalanced or appear listless, they may be suffering from common indigestion. This is not serious if corrected right away. However, if ignored it could lead to permanent damage. You may notice gas bubbles right next to the fish which cause it to float upside down. To cure this, stop feeding fish for a few days. When feeding is resumed, only feed it live food such as *Daphnia*. Prevention can

be established by giving the fish more room to swim by reducing the population of its environment.

If indigestion is allowed to persist unchecked, your fish could suffer from swim-bladder disease. This is more likely to occur in fancy varieties with rounder, fat bodies. It can also be brought about, as are so many other goldfish problems, by overfeeding. The intestines of the fish become overloaded and press against the air-bladder. Once the condition exists in your fish, it will be prone to the problem in the future. Its life can be extended by placing it in a shallow pan with 68°F water deep enough to cover its dorsal fin. Dissolve a small amount of salt or permanganate of potash in the water, renewing it daily. Don't feed the fish for a week; then begin regular feeding with

Any obviously sick fish should be removed from the community immediately for treatment and to keep it from infecting tankmates.

Daphnia, earthworms, scrapes of raw meat and green food. Continue this until a week after fish shows signs of being well.

Another condition which may appear after unchecked indigestion is the shimmies. It can also be brought on by keeping your fish in water that is too cool or by keeping them in water with a high mineral content. You can raise the temperature and treat the fish as you would for common indigestion to effect a cure. Your pet store owner or veterinarian will be able to diagnose various diseases for you if you suspect there is a problem and can describe the condition or take the fish in for examination in person.

Dropsy is a disease that shows itself by having the fish's scales lift free at the edge. This is, unfortunately, an incurable disease brought on, some experts believe, by extended periods in water that is too cold. Serous fluid collects in the tissue spaces and cavities of the fish's body. A fish suffering from dropsy may live for a few months, but many often die immediately.

There are a number of insects that present a threat to your goldfish, especially those living in the outdoor environment of a pool. The best way to protect your fish is to kill these pests on sight. A bug "zapper" stationed near the pool will take care of most of the flying pests. Some of the more common of these pests include dragon fly larva, giant water bugs, hydra, diving beetles, spearmouths, water spiders, etc. Your pet store owner will be able to tell you what measures you need to either kill or prevent the return of any of these particular pests that may invade your pool and endanger your fish. They will also be able to help protect your fish from such dangers as rats, cats, blackbirds and, yes, curious children (*and* adults).

A fish that is this far gone, with clouded eyes and rotted fins, should be humanely sacrificed.

Goldfish Health

Ich is a common parasitic condition. Fortunately, there are a number of very effective medications available for treating it.

Naturally, the best way to make sure your fish stay healthy is to prevent as much disease as possible. As long as you have followed common sense in setting up your aquarium or pool, many of these problems should never arise. You should also remember such other basics as quarantine. Any new fish which you plan to introduce into your pool or aquarium should be placed in a separate tank for at least a week where they can be carefully observed on their own. Similarly, any fish that shows signs of illness or infection should be removed for separate examination and to prevent its problem from spreading to healthy goldfish. The same is true for any new plants you wish to have in with your fish. They should be properly sterilized and placed in quarantine for a time as well.

Normal maintenance and cleaning of your pool or aquarium, careful population control of fish and plant, and regular feedings of proper foods should be enough to prevent most of the diseases that attack goldfish. These actions and a ready knowledge of any problems that *may* arise should keep your goldfish happy, active, and fascinating for many years to come.

The following books by T.F.H. Publications are available at pet shops everywhere.

AQUARIUM PLANTS—
by Dr. K. Rataj and T. Horeman.
ISBN 0-87666-455-9;
TFH H-966, hardcover.
448 pages, 244 color photos, 124 black and white photos.

SUGGESTED READING

A complete volume dealing with aquatic plants, including those for the garden pond. Description and methods of propagation are discussed for each species of plant.

GOLDFISH GUIDE—by Dr. Yoshiichi Matsui.
ISBN 0-87666-545-8; TFH PL-2011
Hardcover. 256 pages, 100 color photos, 38 black and white photos, 14 line illustrations.
Contains information on all aspects of the goldfish; its history, types, biology, ecology, diseases, breeding and genetics, by a Japanese author with more than 50 years of academic and practical experience about goldfish.